27 Christmas Favorites

By Sandy Feldstein

Includes a Play-Along CD in Today's Musical Styles
Accompaniments by David Feldstein

Table of Contents

	Page Number	CD Track
Angels We Have Heard on High	3	1
Away in a Manger	4	2
Bring a Torch, Jeannette, Isabella	5	3
Coventry Carol	6	4
Deck the Hall	7	5
Fum, Fum, Fum	8	6
God Rest You Merry, Gentlemen	9	7
Good King Wenceslaus	10	8
Go Tell It on the Mountain	11	9
Hark! The Herald Angels Sing	12	10
It Came upon the Midnight Clear	13	11
I Saw Three Ships	14	12
Jingle Bells	15	13
Jolly Old Saint Nicholas	16	14
Joy to the World	17	15
O Christmas Tree (O Tannenbaum)	18	16
O Come, All Ye Faithful (Adeste Fideles)	19	17
O Come, O Come, Emmanuel	20	18
O Little Town of Bethlehem	21	19
Pat-A-Pan	22	20
Silent Night	23	21
The First Noel	24	22
The Holly and the Ivy	25	23
The Twelve Days of Christmas	26	24
Up on the Housetop	27	25
We Three Kings of Orient Are	28	26
We Wish You A Merry Christmas	29	27

65 Bleecker Street, New York, NY 10012

Copyright © 2001 by Amidan Music
International Copyright Secured.
All rights reserved including performing rights.
WARNING! This publication is protected by Copyright law. To photocopy or reproduce by
any method is an infringement of the Copyright law. Anyone who reproduces copyrighted
matter is subject to substantial penalties and assessments for each infringement.
Printed in the U.S.A.

ISBN 0-8258-4516-5

ABOUT THE BOOK

This book contains 27 of the world's most famous Christmas carols all written within the comfortable range of your instrument. You can play the songs accompanied by the CD and/or the piano and/or the guitar. Included are chord charts for both the piano and guitar and an instrument fingering chart that covers the notes used in this book.

ABOUT THE CD

All of the songs in this collection are contained on the fully orchestrated CD, which is included in this package. The melody is included softly on each track to help you stay in time with the orchestration. The arrangements are in a variety of traditional and contemporary styles and will add fun and excitement to your holiday season. Put the CD on, and sing and play along, bringing musical cheer to the holiday season.

ANGELS WE HAVE HEARD ON HIGH

Traditional French Tune
Arranged by Sandy Feldstein

2. Shepherds, why this jubilee?
   Why your joyous strains prolong?
   What the gladsome tidings be
   Which inspire your heavenly song?

   Chorus

3. Come to Bethlehem and see
   Him whose birth the angels sing;
   Come, adore on bended knee
   Christ, the Lord, the newborn King.

   Chorus

Copyright © 2001 by Amidan Music

AWAY IN A MANGER

CD TRACK 2

JAMES R. MURRAY
(1841-1905)
Arranged by Sandy Feldstein

1. A-way in a man-ger, no crib for a bed, The lit-tle Lord Je-sus laid down His sweet head; The stars in the sky looked down where He lay, The lit-tle Lord Je-sus, a-sleep on the hay.

2. The cattle are lowing, the poor Baby wakes,
   But little Lord Jesus no crying He makes;
   I love Thee, Lord Jesus, look down from the sky,
   And stay by my cradle till morning is nigh.

3. Be near me, Lord Jesus, I ask Thee to stay
   Close by me forever and love me, I pray;
   Bless all the dear children in Thy tender care,
   And take me to heaven to live with Thee there.

BRING A TORCH, JEANNETTE, ISABELLA

CD TRACK 3

Traditional French Carol
Arranged by Sandy Feldstein

1. Bring a torch, Jeannette, Isabella,
Bring a torch and quickly run.
Christ is born good folk of the village,
Christ is born and Mary's calling,
Ah! Ah! beautiful is the Mother,
Ah! Ah! beautiful is her Son.

2. Quiet all nor waken Jesus, quiet all and whisper low,
Silence all, and gather around Him, talk and noise might waken Jesus,
Hush, hush, quietly now He slumbers, hush, hush, quietly now He sleeps.

Come and see within the stable, come and see the Holy One,
Come and see the lovely Jesus, white His brow, His cheeks are rosy.
Hush, hush, quietly now He slumbers, hush, hush, quietly now He sleeps

French:
Un flambeau, Jeannette, Isabella, Un flambeau, Courons au berceau.
C'est Jésus, bones gens du hameau, Le Christ est né, Marie appelle.
Ah! Ah! Ah! que la Mére est belle!
Ah! Ah! Ah! que l'Enfant est beau.

Copyright © 2001 by Amidan Music

CD TRACK 5
DECK THE HALL

Traditional Welsh Carol
Arranged by Sandy Feldstein

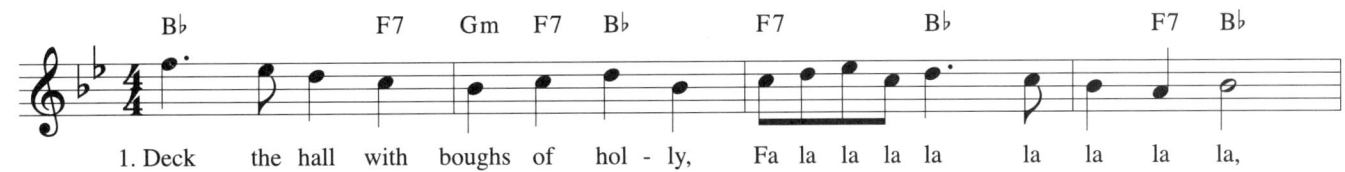
1. Deck the hall with boughs of hol - ly, Fa la la la la la la la la,

'Tis the sea - son to be jol - ly, Fa la la la la la la la la;

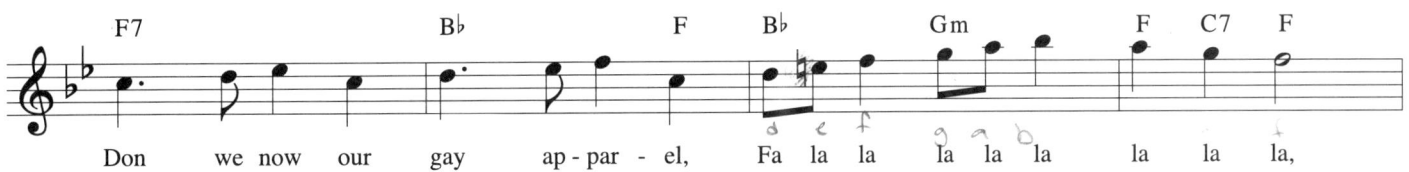
Don we now our gay ap - par - el, Fa la la la la la la la la,

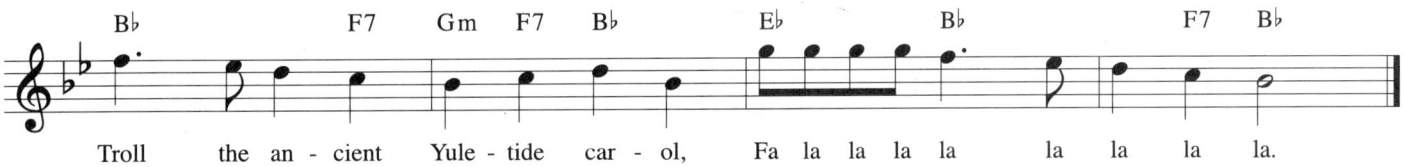
Troll the an - cient Yule - tide car - ol, Fa la la la la la la la la.

2. See the blazing Yule before us,
   Fa la la la la la la la la,
   Strike the harp and join the chorus,
   Fa la la la la la la la la;
   Follow me in merry measure,
   Fa la la la la la la la la,
   While I tell of Yuletide treasure,
   Fa la la la la la la la la.

3. Fast away the old year passes,
   Fa la la la la la la la la,
   Hail the new, ye lads and lasses,
   Fa la la la la la la la la;
   Sing we joyous all together,
   Fa la la la la la la la la,
   Heedless of the wind and weather,
   Fa la la la la la la la la.

Copyright © 2001 by Amidan Music

FUM, FUM, FUM

Arranged by Sandy Feldstein

2. Thanks to God for holidays, sing "Fum, fum, fum."
   Thanks to God for holidays, sing "Fum, fum, fum."
   Now we all our voices raise, And sing a song of grateful praise,
   Celebrate in song and story, all the wonders of His glory,
   Fum, fum, fum.

Copyright © 2001 by Amidan Music

GOD REST YOU MERRY, GENTLEMEN

William Sandy's *Christmas Carols Ancient and Modern*

Traditional English Tune
Arranged by Sandy Feldstein

1. God rest you mer-ry, gen-tle-men, Let noth-ing you dis-may, Re-mem-ber Christ our Sav-ior was born on Christ-mas day, To save us all from Sa-tan's pow'r when we were gone a-stray. O____ tid-ings of com-fort and joy, com-fort and joy, O____ Tid-ings of com-fort and joy.

2. From God our heavenly Father
   A blessed angel came,
   And unto certain shepherds
   Brought tidings of the same,
   How that in Bethlehem was born
   The son of God by name,
   O, tidings of comfort and joy,
   Comfort and joy,
   O, tidings of comfort and joy.

3. "Fear not, then," said the angel,
   "Let nothing you affright,
   This day is born a Saviour
   Of a pure Virgin bright,
   To free all those who trust in Him
   From Satan's power and might."
   O, tidings of comfort and joy,
   Comfort and joy,
   O, tidings of comfort and joy.

Copyright © 2001 by Amidan Music

GOOD KING WENCESLAUS

John M. Neale

Theodoricus Petrus of Nyland's *Piae Cantiones* 1592
Arranged by Sandy Feldstein

1. Good King Wen-ces-laus looked out, On the Feast of Ste-phen,

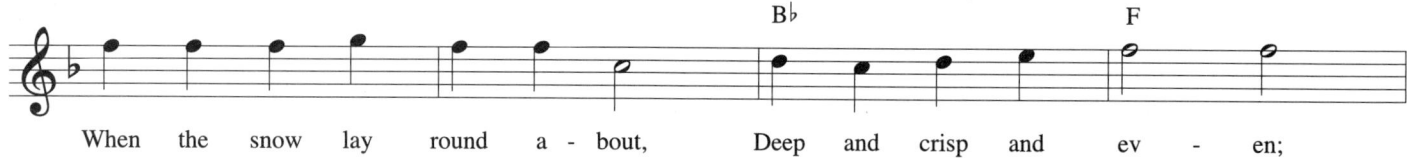

When the snow lay round a-bout, Deep and crisp and ev-en;

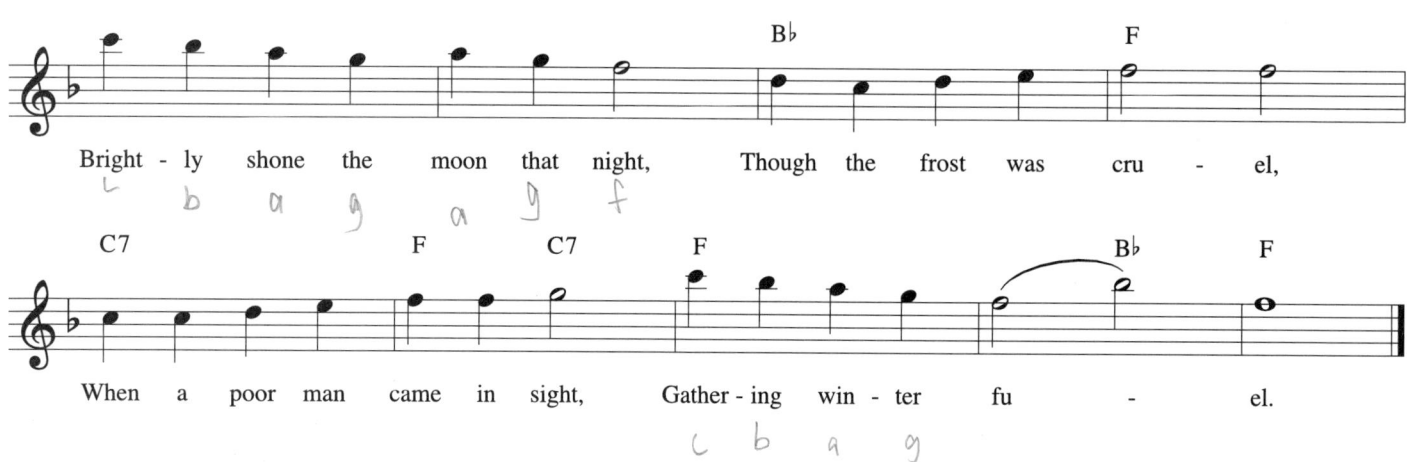

Bright-ly shone the moon that night, Though the frost was cru-el,

When a poor man came in sight, Gath-er-ing win-ter fu-el.

2. "Hither, page, and stand by me,
   If thou knowest it, telling,
   Yonder peasant, who is he,
   Where and what his dwelling?"
   "Sire, he lives a good league hence
   Underneath the mountain,
   Right against the forest fence
   By Saint Agnes' fountain."

3. "Bring me flesh, and bring me wine,
   Bring me pine logs hither,
   Thou and I will see him dine
   When we bear them thither."
   Page and monarch forth they went,
   Forth they went together,
   Through the rude wind's wild lament
   And the bitter weather.

4. "Sire, the night is darker now,
   And the wind blows stronger;
   Fails my heart, I know not how,
   I can go no longer."
   "Mark my footsteps, my good page,
   Tread thou in them boldly,
   Thou shalt find the winter's rage
   Freeze thy blood less coldly."

5. In his master's steps he trod,
   Where the snow lay dinted,
   Heat was in the very sod
   Which the saint had printed.
   Therefore, Christian men, be sure,
   Wealth or rank possessing,
   Ye who now will bless the poor
   Shall yourselves find blessing.

GO TELL IT ON THE MOUNTAIN

Arranged by Sandy Feldstein

2. He made me a watchman upon the city wall,
   And if I serve Him truly, I am the least of all.

   Chorus

3. In the time of David, some said he was a king,
   And if a child is true born, the Lord will hear him sing.

   Chorus

HARK! THE HERALD ANGELS SING

Charles Wesley

FELIX MENDELSSOHN BARTHOLDY
(1809-1847)
Arranged by Sandy Feldstein

1. Hark! the herald angels sing, Glory to the new-born King;
Peace on earth and mercy mild, God and sinners reconciled!
Joyful all ye nations rise, Join the triumph of the skies;
With th'angelic hosts proclaim, Christ is born in Bethlehem.

Refrain
Hark! the herald angels sing, Glory to the new-born King!

2. Christ, by highest heav'n adored,
   Christ, the everlasting Lord;
   Late in time behold Him come,
   Offspring of the Virgin's womb.
   Veiled in flesh the Godhead see;
   Hail th'Incarnate Deity,
   Pleased as man with man to dwell,
   Jesus our Emmanuel!

3. Mild He lays His glory by,
   Born that man no more may die,
   Born to raise the sons of earth,
   Born to give them second birth.
   Ris'n with healing in His wings,
   Light and life to all He brings,
   Hail the Sun of Righteousness!
   Hail, the heav'n born Prince of Peace!

IT CAME UPON THE MIDNIGHT CLEAR

Edward Hamilton Sears

RICHARD STORRS WILLIS
(1819-1900)
Arranged by Sandy Feldstein

1. It came upon the midnight clear, That glorious song of old, From angels bending near the earth To touch their harps of gold. "Peace on the earth good will to men, From heav'ns all gracious King." The world in solemn stillness lay To hear the angels sing.

2. Still through the cloven skies they come
   With peaceful wings unfurled,
   And still their heav'nly music floats
   O'er all the weary world.
   Above its sad and lowly plains
   They bend on hov'ring wing,
   And ever o'er its Babel sounds
   The blessed angels sing.

3. O ye, beneath life's crushing load,
   Whose forms are bending low.
   Who toil along the climbing way
   With painful steps and slow,
   Look now, for glad and golden hours
   Come swiftly on the wing,
   O rest beside the weary road
   And hear the angels sing.

4. For lo! the days are hast'ning on,
   By prophets seen of old,
   When with the evercircling years
   Shall come the time foretold,
   When the new heav'n and earth shall own
   The Prince of Peace their King,
   And the whole world send back the song
   Which now the angels sing.

Copyright © 2001 by Amidan Music

I SAW THREE SHIPS

CD TRACK 12

Arranged by Sandy Feldstein

1. I saw three ships come sail-ing in on Christ-mas Day, on Christ-mas Day, I saw three ships come sail-ing in on Christ-mas Day in the morn-ing.

2. And what was in those ships all three?
   The Virgin Mary and Christ were there
   Pray whither sailed those ships all three?
   O they sailed into Bethlehem.

3. And all the bells on earth shall ring
   And all the angels in heaven shall sing,
   And all the souls on earth shall sing
   Then let us all rejoice amain.

Copyright © 2001 by Amidan Music

JINGLE BELLS

JAMES PIERPONT
Arranged by Sandy Feldstein

2. A day or two ago, I thought I'd take a ride,
   And soon Miss Fannie Bright was seated by my side;
   The horse was lean and lank, misfortune seemed his lot,
   He got into a drifted bank, and we, we got upsot.

   Chorus

3. Now the ground is white, go it while you're young,
   Take the girls tonight, and sing this sleighing song;
   Just get a bobtailed nag, two-forty for his speed,
   Then hitch him to an open sleigh, and crack! You'll take the lead.

   Chorus

CD TRACK 14

JOLLY OLD SAINT NICHOLAS

Traditional
Arranged by Sandy Feldstein

1. Jol - ly old Saint Nich - o - las, Lean your ear this way!

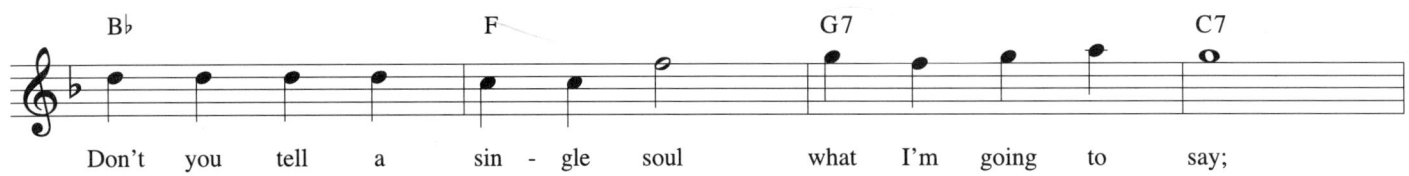
Don't you tell a sin - gle soul what I'm going to say;

Christ - mas Eve is com - ing soon; Now, you dear old man,

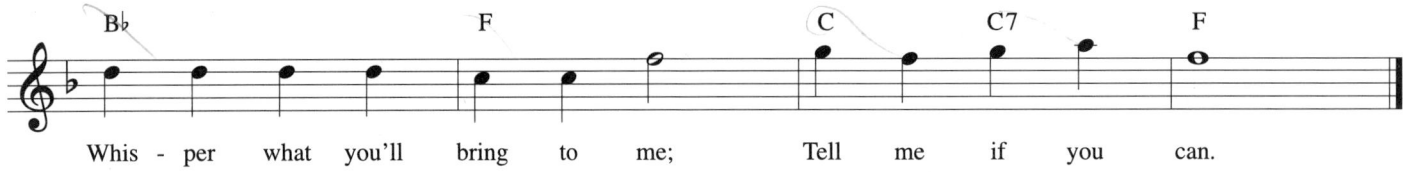
Whis - per what you'll bring to me; Tell me if you can.

2. When the clock is striking twelve,
   When I'm fast asleep,
   Down the chimney broad and black
   With your pack you'll creep;
   All the stockings you will find
   Hanging in a row,
   Mine will be the shortest one,
   You'll be sure to know.

3. Johnny wants a pair of skates;
   Susy wants a dolly;
   Nellie wants a story book,
   She thinks dolls are folly;
   As for me, my little brain
   Isn't very bright;
   Choose for me, Dear Santa Claus,
   What you think is right.

Copyright © 2001 by Amidan Music

JOY TO THE WORLD

GEORGE FRIDERIC HANDEL
(1685-1759)
Arranged by Sandy Feldstein

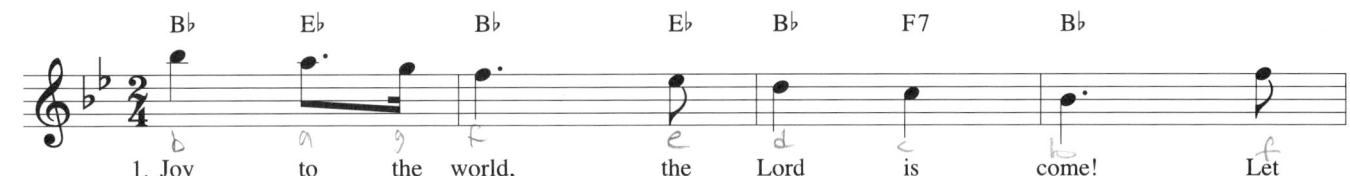

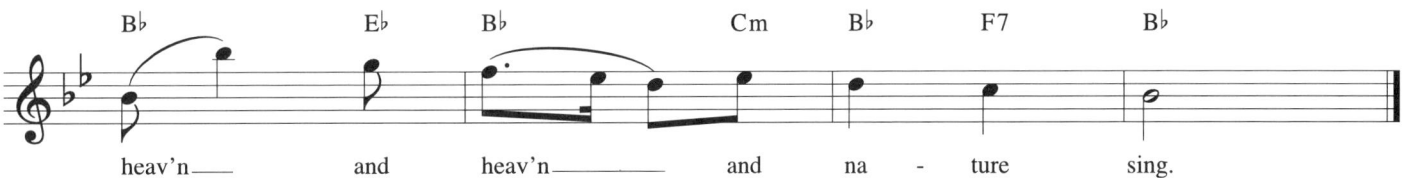

2. Joy to the world, the Savior reigns! Let men their songs employ;
   While fields and flood, rocks, hills and plains,
   Repeat the sounding joy, repeat the sounding joy,
   Repeat, repeat the sounding joy.

3. He rules the world with truth and grace, and makes the nations prove
   The glories of His righteousness,
   And wonders of His love, and wonders of His love,
   And wonders and wonders of His love.

O CHRISTMAS TREE
(O Tannenbaum)

Traditional German Carol
Arranged by Sandy Feldstein

German:
O Tannenbaum, O Tannenbaum,
Wie treu sind deine Blatter!
O Tannenbaum, O Tannenbaum,
Wie treu sind deine Blatter!

Du Grunst nicht nur zur Sommerzeit,
Nein auch im Winter, wenn es schneit.
O Tannenbaum, O Tannenbaum,
Wie treu sind deine Blatter!

O COME, ALL YE FAITHFUL
(Adeste Fideles)

CD TRACK 17

Words and Music by **JOHN F. WADE**
(1711-1786)
Arranged by Sandy Feldstein

2. Sing choirs of Angels, sing in exaltation,
   Sing, all ye citizens of heaven above;
   Glory to God, In the highest glory,
   O come, let us adore Him, O come, let us adore Him,
   O come, let us adore Him, Christ, the Lord.

3. Yea, Lord, we greet Thee, born this happy morning,
   Jesus, to Thee be all glory given;
   Word of the Father now in flesh appearing,
   O come, let us adore Him, O come, let us adore Him,
   O come, let us adore Him, Christ, the Lord.

Latin:
Adeste fideles, laeti triumphantes, Venite, venite in Bethlehem.
Natum videte, Regem angelrum, Venite, adoremus,
Venite, adoremus, Venite, adoremus Dominum.

Copyright © 2001 by Amidan Music

O COME, O COME, EMMANUEL

Adapted from plainsong by Thomas Helmore
Arranged by Sandy Feldstein

2. O come, Thou Wisdom from on high, and order all things, far and nigh,
   To us the path of knowledge show, and cause us in her ways to go.

   Chorus

3. O come, Desire of Nations, bind all peoples in one heart and mind,
   Bid envy, strife, and quarrels cease, fill the whole world with heaven's peace.

   Chorus

O LITTLE TOWN OF BETHLEHEM

Phillips Brooks

LEWIS H. REDNER
(1831-1908)
Arranged by Sandy Feldstein

2. For Christ is born of Mary and gathered all above
   While mortals sleep, the angels keep their watch of wondering love.
   O morning stars, together proclaim the holy birth,
   And praises sing to God the King and peace to men on earth.

3. How silently, how silently the wondrous gift is given,
   So God imparts to human hearts the blessings of his heaven.
   No ear may hear His coming, but in this world of sin,
   Where meek souls will receive Him, still the dear Christ enters in.

4. O holy Child of Bethlehem descend to us, we pray,
   Cast out our sin and enter in, be born in us today.
   We hear the Christmas angels the great glad tidings tell,
   O come to us, abide with us our Lord Emmanuel!

PAT-A-PAN

Arranged by Sandy Feldstein

1. Will ye bring the lit-tle drum, Will ye bring the fife and come, Make ye mer-ry as ye play. Tu-re-lu-re-lu. Pat-a-pat-a-pan. Make ye mer-ry as ye play for it is the Ho-ly Day.

2. As your father did before,
   Will ye bring the fife once more
   And be merry as ye play.
   Tu re lu re lu. Pat-a-pat-a-pan.
   Make ye merry as ye play for it is the Holy Day.

3. Will ye let the praises ring,
   Will ye let the bagpipe sing,
   Leave your labors as they lay.
   Tu re lu re lu. Pat-a-pat-a-pan.
   Leave your labors as they lay for it is the Holy Day.

Copyright © 2001 by Amidan Music

SILENT NIGHT

CD TRACK 21

Joseph Mohr

FRANZ GRUBER
(1787-1863)
Arranged by Sandy Feldstein

2. Silent night, holy night!
   Shepherds quake at the sight.
   Glories stream from heaven afar,
   Heavenly hosts sing, "Alleluia!"
   Christ, the Savior is born,
   Christ, the Savior is born.

3. Silent night, holy night!
   Son of God, love's pure light!
   Radiant beams from Thy holy face
   With the dawn of redeeming grace,
   Jesus, Lord at Thy birth,
   Jesus, Lord at Thy birth.

THE FIRST NOEL

Traditional English Carol
Arranged by Sandy Feldstein

2. They looked up and saw a star
   Shining in the east beyond them far,
   And to the earth it gave great light,
   And so it continued both day and night;
   Noel, Noel, Noel, Noel,
   Born is the King of Israel!

3. And by the light of that same star
   Three Wise Men came from a country afar,
   To seek for a king was their intent,
   And to follow the star where'er it went;
   Noel, Noel, Noel, Noel,
   Born is the King of Israel!

Copyright © 2001 by Amidan Music

THE HOLLY AND THE IVY

Traditional English Carol
Arranged by Sandy Feldstein

2. The holly bears a prickle as sharp as any thorn,
   And Mary bore sweet Jesus Christ, on Christmas day in the morn;
   The holly bears a berry as red as any blood,
   And Mary bore sweet Jesus Christ to do poor sinners good;
   The holly bears a blossom as white as any flower,
   And Mary bore sweet Jesus Christ to be the dear Savior.

Copyright © 2001 by Amidan Music

THE TWELVE DAYS OF CHRISTMAS

CD TRACK 24

Traditional English Song
Arranged by Sandy Feldstein

1. On the first day of Christ-mas my true love sent to me A par-tridge in a pear tree.
2. On the sec-ond day of Christ-mas my true love sent to me two tur-tle doves, and a par-tridge in a pear tree.
3. On the third (etc.) three French hens,
4. On the fourth (etc.) four call-ing birds,*
5. On the fifth day of Christ-mas my true love sent to me, five gold-en rings, four call-ing birds, three French hens, two tur-tle doves, and a par-tridge in a pear tree.
6. On the sixth day of Christ-mas my true love sent to me, six geese a-lay-ing,
   seven swans a-swim-ming,
   eight maids a-milk-ing,
   nine la-dies danc-ing,
   ten lords a-leap-ing,
   eleven pip-ers pip-ing,
   twelve drum-mers drum-ming,
   three French hens, two tur-tle doves, and a par-tridge in a pear tree.

*Sing in reverse order on repeats.

Copyright © 2001 by Amidan Music

UP ON THE HOUSETOP

CD TRACK 25

B. R. HANBY
Arranged by Sandy Feldstein

2. First comes the stocking of little Nell, oh, dear Santa, fill it well,
   Give her a dolly that laughs and cries, one that can open and close its eyes.

   Chorus

3. Here is the stocking of little Will, look at what a glorious fill,
   Here is a hammer and lots of tacks, bat and a ball and a whip that cracks.

   Chorus

Copyright © 2001 by Amidan Music

WE THREE KINGS OF ORIENT ARE

JOHN H. HOPKINS
(1820-1891)
Arranged by Sandy Feldstein

1. We three kings of Orient are, Bearing gifts we traverse afar, Field and fountain, moor and mountain, Following yonder star.

Chorus
Oh, star of wonder, star of night, Star with royal beauty bright, Westward leading, still proceeding, Guide us to the perfect Light.

2. Born a babe on Bethlehem's plain,
   Gold I bring to crown Him again;
   King forever, ceasing never
   Over us all to reign.

   Chorus

3. Frankincense to offer have I;
   Incense owns a Deity nigh,
   Prayer and praising all men raising,
   Worship Him, God on high.

   Chorus

4. Myrrh is mine; its bitter perfume,
   Breathes a life of gathering gloom;
   Sorrowing, sighing, bleeding, dying,
   Sealed in the stone-cold tomb.

   Chorus

5. Glorious now, behold Him arise,
   King and God and Sacrifice;
   Heaven sings "Hallelujah!"
   "Hallelujah!" earth replies.

   Chorus

Copyright © 2001 by Amidan Music

WE WISH YOU A MERRY CHRISTMAS

Arranged by Sandy Feldstein

2. Please bring us some figgy pudding, please bring us some figgy pudding,
   Please bring us some figgy pudding, please bring it right here.

   Chorus

3. We won't leave until we get some, we won't leave until we get some,
   We won't leave until we get some, please bring it right here.

   Chorus

Copyright © 2001 by Amidan Music

FLUTE FINGERING CHART FOR THIS BOOK

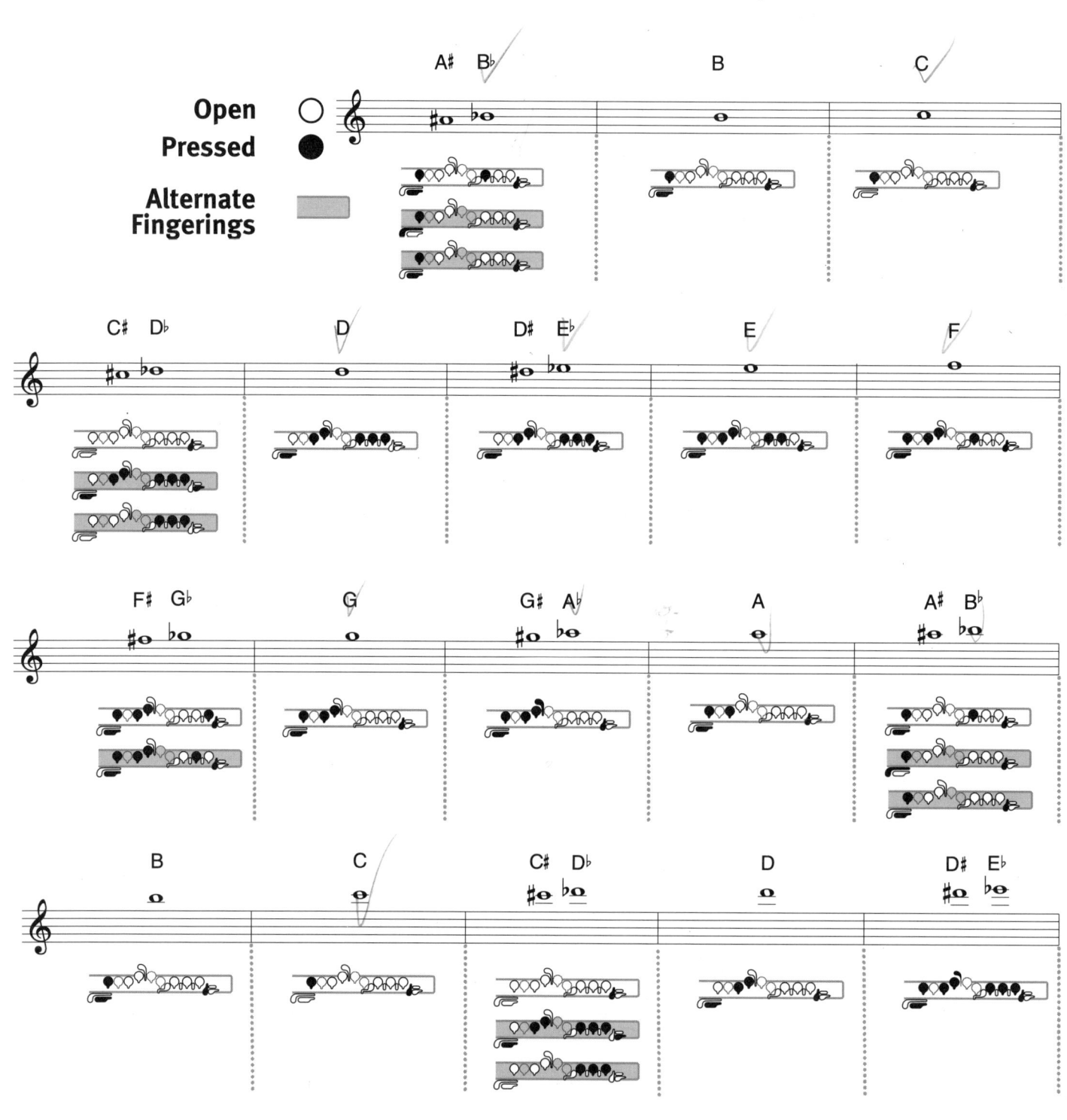

PIANO FINGERING CHART FOR THIS BOOK

A♭
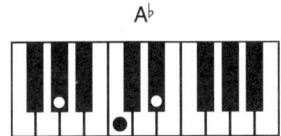

A7

Am
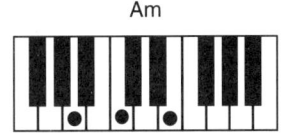

B♭
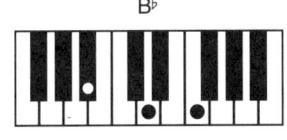

B♭7
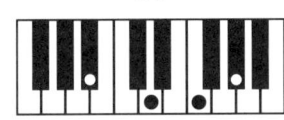

B♭dim
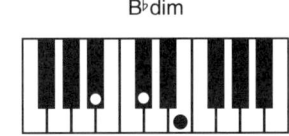

B

C7
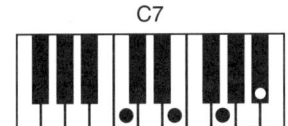

Cm
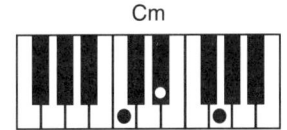

Cdim
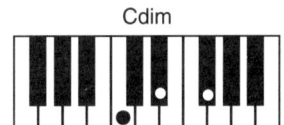

D♭
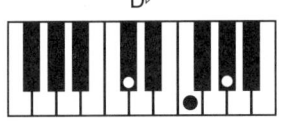

D7
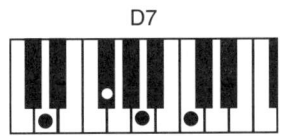

Dm
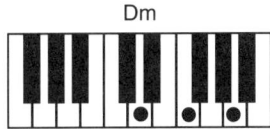

E♭
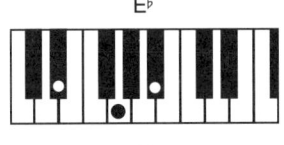

E♭7
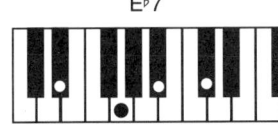

E♭dim
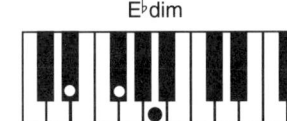

F

F7
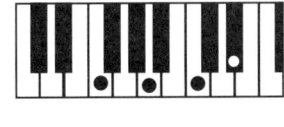

Fm
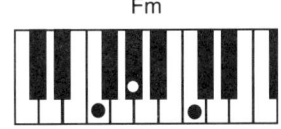

G
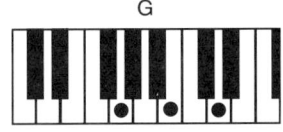

G7
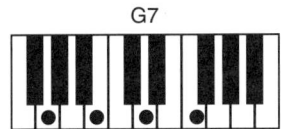

Gm
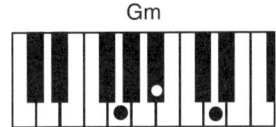

GUITAR FINGERING CHART FOR THIS BOOK

Ab
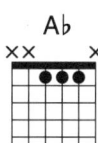

A7
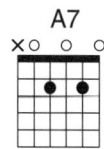

Am
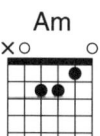

Bb
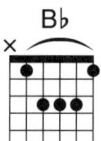

Bb7
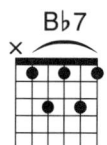

Bbdim

C7
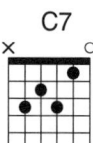

Cm
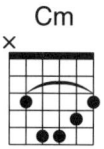

Db
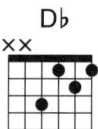

D7
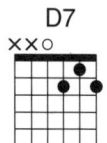

Dm

Eb7
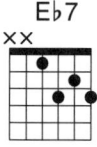

Ebdim
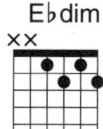

F
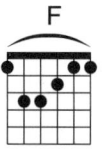

F7

Fm

G

G7

Gm